A Dance to Rem

Lorna Liverpool
Illustrated by
Sarah-Louise Hibbs

Published by © Lorna Liverpool 2014

ISBN: 978-0-9929047-0-8

Printed by Tien Wah Press SDN BHD.
A member of DAI NIPPON Group of Companies
89, Jalan Tampoi, Kawasan Perindustrian Tampoi,
81300 Johor Bahru, Johor Darul Takzim, Malaysia.

I dedicate this book to my beloved sister Ros who I love and miss so very much.

This book belongs to

....

Today was the last day of rehearsals for tomorrow's Festival of Dance in the park, making the dance studio incredibly busy. The boys: George, William, Carl and Baba were practising their routines for the last time; they were hitting their ng'oma drums hard.

Excitement, happiness and confidence filled the air. I was practising my African dance routine with my best friends: Marcia, Rema and three other dancers. For some unknown reason I kept getting my dance steps wrong, which was not like me at all.

Miss Okeybaya, our dance teacher came over to me.
"Kaa'hina," she said, "You must not worry so much, it
is natural to feel a little nervous before an event. It will
be alright tomorrow, okay?"
"Yes, Miss Okeybaya," I replied, glumly.

"Kaa'hina!" As I turned around I saw my mum approaching. "How did you get on today?" she asked, as she planted a kiss on my forehead.
"Not so well today, Mum. I was getting my steps wrong all the time," I said, as tears started trickling down my cheeks.
"Everything is going to be alright tomorrow," Mum said, giving me a huge bear hug.
"I know you can do it, believe in yourself."
After that I felt a little better.

As I laid on my bed that night, thinking about the next
day's dance performance, Mum and Dad walked in.
Mum was holding a small wooden box in her hands.
"Mum, what if I get my dance steps all wrong again?" I
said nervously. I could feel the tears coming again.
Dad then said, "You are going to be brilliant, beyond
brilliant on the day Kaa'hina. You wait and see!"
Mum walked towards me and handed me the box.
As I opened it, I saw something sparkle; it was
Grandma's beautiful gold chain. It was the colourful
stones that sparkled, like the sun rays on the Nile.

I quickly jumped up with excitement. Mum and Dad gave me a huge hug.

"This used to be Grandma's favourite chain," I said.

"Yes, it was Grandma's special chain. The ankh symbol represents the key to eternal life. This chain has been in the family for hundreds of years," Mum replied.

"Wow Mum!" I said. "That is a long time."

"That is true," Mum replied.
"Your Grandma Pea wanted us to give you this special chain when the time was right. Your dad and I thought it would be lovely if you wore it at the dance performance tomorrow. I know your Grandma Pea would have loved that."

As I snuggled up in bed that night, wearing Grandma Pea's special chain, I couldn't stop thinking about her and wishing she was here. As I held my ankh chain, all of a sudden the large stone in the middle started to glow bright green. I quickly turned on my bedside lamp because I couldn't believe what I was seeing.

As I took off the chain, it fell on the floor. The green glow was becoming more and more dazzling. The large stone in the middle of the ankh had vanished and in its place was a dark green and black vortex, swirling round and round, faster and faster, expanding by the minute. I jumped off the bed to touch the black vortex but was pulled in by the swirling force.

Before I could scream for help, I found myself in the most beautiful enchanted garden I had ever seen. There were birds singing away, and lots of colourful butterflies flying around an oak tree. One of the butterflies landed on my shoulder. It had bright lights around the edge of its wings. "Wow! This is so magical," I thought. Everywhere I looked there were sights I had never seen before: exotic flowers, unusual birds and green grass, bright and vibrant.

I turned around and saw an old lady walking towards me. She was dressed in a lovely gown and was holding a gold walking stick, with a large ankh on the top of it. She came up to me and greeted me. "We have been waiting for you", she said, "I am one of the Ancient Ones, Kaa'hina. I want to take you to a special lake for you to watch some African dancing.

Hold my hand tight and don't let go!"
With a thud, she banged her golden stick on the
ground three times, and we began to fly high
up in the sky.
"Wow!" I shrieked with excitement. I could feel
butterflies in my stomach. I couldn't believe this
was actually happening to me.

We flew over a lake which had nine large crystals rotating on it. Each crystal had an old lady levitating above it, except for two. They were all wearing beautiful, colourful African outfits. On the grass area were three men kneeling down with large ng'oma drums in front of them.

We landed above the crystal in the middle of the circle. The old lady that had brought me here flew away. All the old ladies levitating above their crystals greeted me, and said, "We are your great grandmothers, going back hundreds of years. We are known as the Ancient Ones."

"Kaa'hina, watch us perform this African dance and learn."

As I looked at my grandmothers I realised they were all wearing the same kind of ankh chain that Grandma Pea had left me. As the drums started to play, the old ladies began to dance in harmony with the drums moving swiftly and gracefully as one. As they danced their crystals generated a glow, bright green in colour. It was so amazing; I was so overwhelmed.
A feeling of tranquillity swept over me; I knew then that I could do my dance performance in the park the next day. I was now confident.

The great grandmothers had now finished
their dance and flew towards me.
Forming a circle around me, they held hands and
bowed. "You are an extension of us. All that we
can do, you can do. Trust in yourself. We will always
be with you, Kaa'hina. We love you so much".
With that, they disappeared into
the lake with the crystals.

But not all of them were gone. Grandma Pea appeared from nowhere, and gave me a kiss on my forehead and a big bear hug, just like she always did. I wrapped myself around her and cried. I didn't want to let her go.

Grandma then said in her soft voice, "I love you so very much Kaa'hina," as she wiped my tears away. "I am so proud of you taking part in your dance performance tomorrow, I will always be with you," she said.

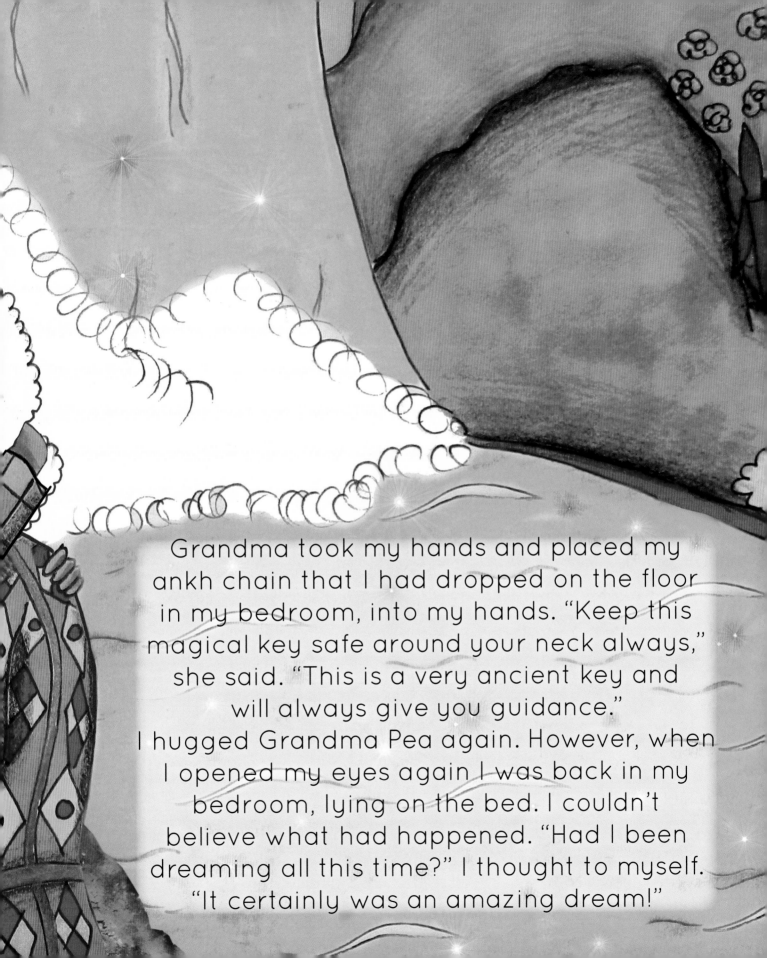

Grandma took my hands and placed my ankh chain that I had dropped on the floor in my bedroom, into my hands. "Keep this magical key safe around your neck always," she said. "This is a very ancient key and will always give you guidance."
I hugged Grandma Pea again. However, when I opened my eyes again I was back in my bedroom, lying on the bed. I couldn't believe what had happened. "Had I been dreaming all this time?" I thought to myself. "It certainly was an amazing dream!"

The next morning was the day of my performance. I arrived at the Festival of Dance; there was a buzz in the air, an atmosphere of excitement.

I could see Marcia, Rema and the boys all together, waving at me. I went over to them, and we had a group hug.
Marcia said, "We'd better get changed now".

I had finished putting my African costume on when my dance teacher, Miss Okeybaya came over to me and said, with a smile on her face, "You are going to be brilliant today, Kaa'hina. Just do your best."
"Yes, I am going to do my best Miss Okeybaya," I replied. I held my ankh chain, which made me feel closer to Grandma Pea.

It was time for our group to go onto the stage. As I walked onto the stage hundreds of people were clapping. I could see Mummy and Daddy, in the front looking really happy and waving to us all. We got into position as the African drums started to play. I quickly glanced at my ankh chain; a green glow appeared.

I then realised that it was not a dream that I had the night before. It was real! I really knew then that my great grandmothers were watching over me as I performed my dance. The dance group and I moved as one, twisting and twirling to the rhythm of the drum beat. I felt excited and very confident. The drums started playing faster and faster as we stamped our feet. The audience cheered and were clapping their hands with admiration.

Everyone was feeling happy. I was feeling happy. I again glanced at my ankh chain, but this time the glow had disappeared. I wasn't worried though, as I now knew that whenever I felt worried or scared all I had to do was hold my ankh chain and my grandmas would always be there with me.

QUESTIONS

1. Why was Kaa'hina feeling glum during her dance rehearsal?

2. Kaa'hina's mum handed her a box. What was inside?

3. When Kaa'hina touched the vortex in her bedroom what happened?

4. Kaa'hina was in the enchanted garden, kneeling down, when something landed on her shoulder. What was it?

5. The old lady in the enchanted garden banged her golden stick three times. What happened after that?

6. Did Kaa'hina find the confidence that she needed to perform at the dance festival?